My Flight Suit Pocket

is dedicated to all of the awesome
military kids out there (and their moms)

Find more, including additional note and
drawing pages to fill **your** flight suit pocket as
well as a Dad Edition of this book, at
BrainExecutiveProgram.com/MyPocket

AF425678

My mom is in the military.

That means she works to help keep our country and the whole world safe.

She has a really special job,
so she wears a flight suit.

A flight suit is a big, green uniform

that sort of looks like jammies.

She wears it because she is a pilot, a flight officer, an aircraft mechanic, a flight surgeon, or does any other job that requires her to fly.

She flies in huge planes,

agile helicopters,

or even really fast jets.

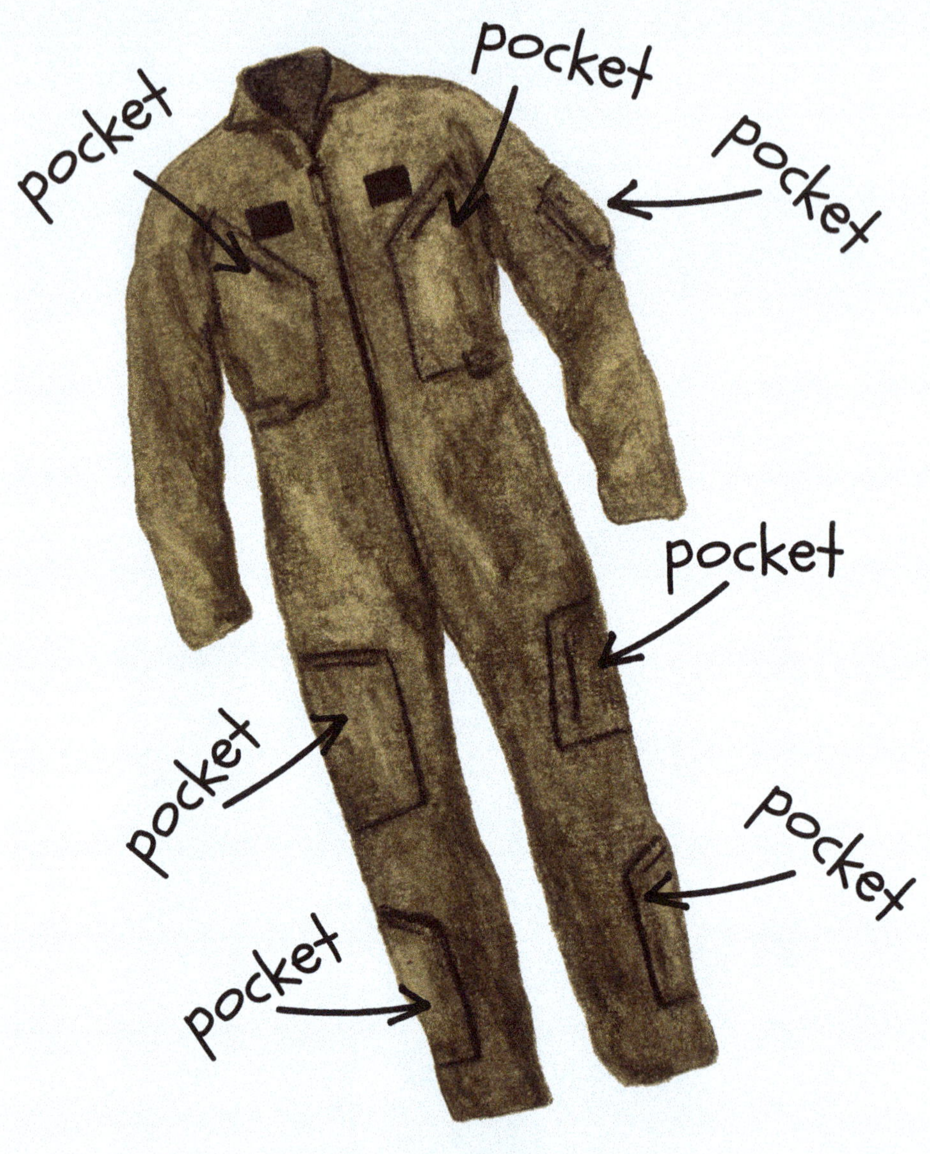

My mom's flight suit has a lot of pockets.

This pocket is for pens and lip balm.

This pocket is for her wallet and hair ties.

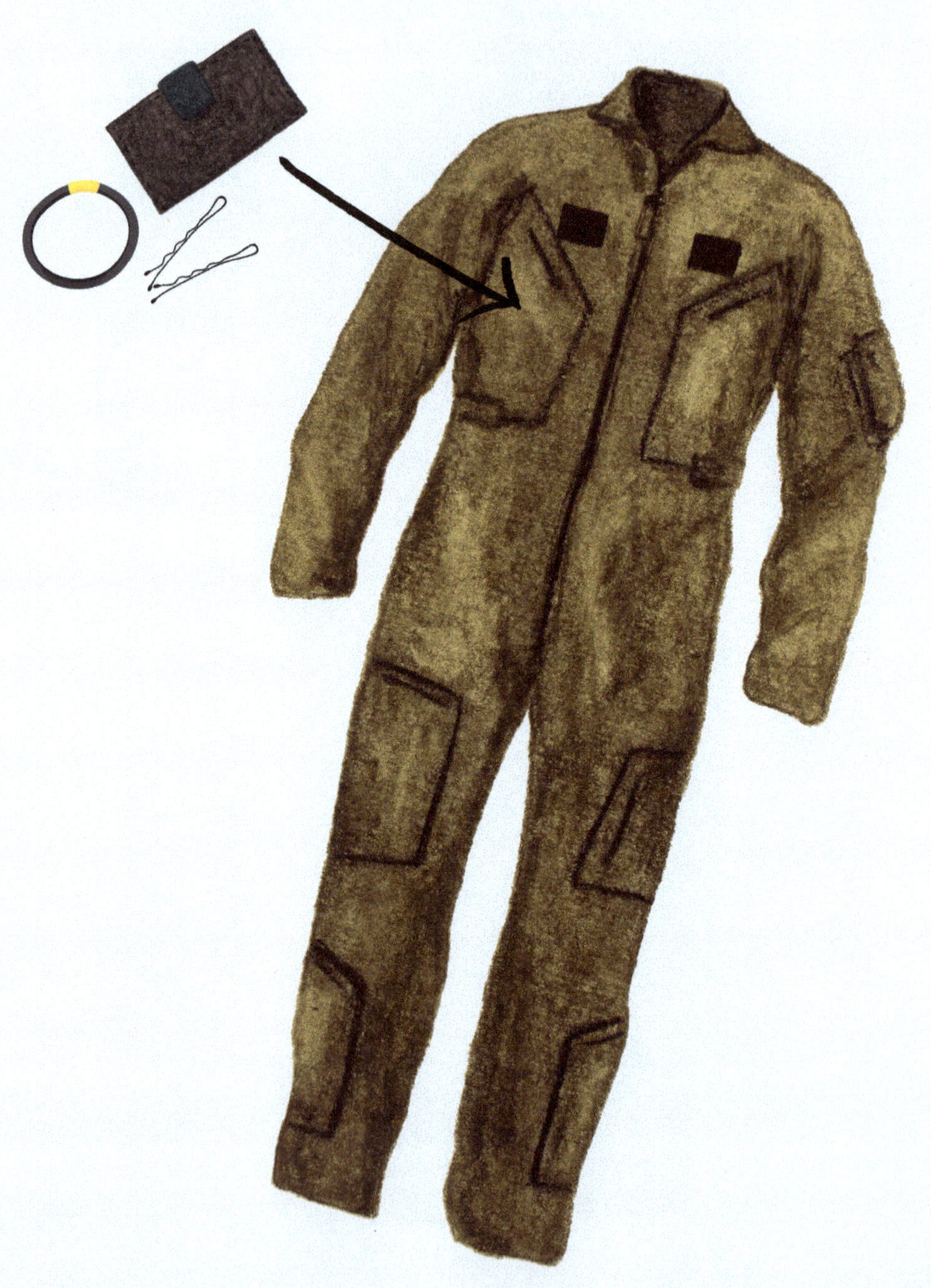

She keeps a special hat
called a cover in this pocket,

and in this pocket
she keeps snacks.

My mom has one pocket that is really special.

She gave it to me. It's **my** flight suit pocket.

Sometimes my mom has to be gone for a really long time because of her job.

When that happens, I miss her a lot.

I wish I could go with her,

but she says that kids are not allowed.

That is why she gave one of her
flight suit pockets to me.

It's a special pocket that I put
things in just for her.

Sometimes I give my mom notes
and cards to put in my pocket.

Sometimes I make her drawings
or give her photos.

Sometimes I even find small things to send
her like a tiny rock I found at the park
or a shell from the beach.

It makes me feel better
that even when my
mom is far away,

she has something with her that is from me.

She says that it makes us feel close,

even when we are far apart.

Having a mom in the military
is really special.

My mom says that I help keep the
whole world safe

by letting her go to work.

And while we are far apart, I know that she has something from me close to her heart,

in **my** flight suit pocket.

Dear Mommy,

Me and Mom

Dear Mommy,

My Family

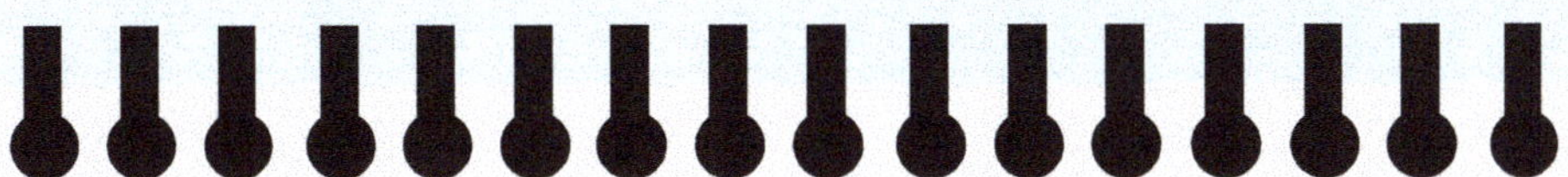

Hi Mom,

www.ingramcontent.com/pod-product-compliance
Lightning Source LLC
Chambersburg PA
CBHW040139150726
48005CB00015B/2564